TENNIS
Handbook

 HANCOCK HOUSE PUBLISHERS

ISBN 0-88839-047-5

Copyright © 1980 Lajoie, Robert &
Lajoie, Gesele

Cataloguing in Publication Data
Lajoie, Robert & Lajoie, Gesele
    Tennis handbook and curriculum guide
(Physical education series)

    Bibliography: p.
    ISBN 0-88839-043-2 pa.
    1. Tennis - Training. I. Title.
II. Series: Physical Education Series (North
Vancouver, B.C.)
GV1017.H7J6   796.35'5'0712   C80-091140-7

All rights reserved. No part of this publication may be reproduced,
stored in a retrieval system or transmitted in any form or by any
means, electronic, mechanical, photocopying, recording or otherwise
without the prior written permission of Hancock House Publishers.

Editor Barbara Herringer
Design & Production Paul Willies
Cover Photo Paul Bond
Typeset by Donna White *in Megaron type on an AM Varityper Comp/Edit*

Second Printing 1982

Published by
HANCOCK HOUSE PUBLISHERS
1431 Harrison Avenue, Blaine, WA, U.S.A. 98230
256 Route 81, Killingworth, CT, U.S.A. 06417
HANCOCK HOUSE PUBLISHERS LTD.
19313 Zero Avenue, Surrey, B.C., Canada V3S 5J9

Table of Contents

Acknowledgments ....
Chapter One
Format and Purpose of the Handbook
    A. Introduction.. 5
    B. Purpose of the Handbook 5
    C. Handbook Format 5
    D. Objectives of the Program.. 5
    E. Application to Classroom Teaching 5
    F. Description of the Levels Approach................................... 6
    G. Explanation of the Activity Sequence Chart......................... 6
    H. Activity Sequence Chart.. 7
    I. Relationship of Tennis to Goals and Learning Outcomes........ 7

Chapter Two
Skill Development and Teaching Techniques
    A. Basic Skills 8
        1. Ball Control and Racquet Skills 8
        2. Footwork 11
        3. Ball Pick-up 12
    B. Individual Skills 12
        1. Forehand Groundstroke 12
        2. Backhand Groundstroke...14
        3. Forehand and Backhand: Common Errors and Stroke Correction ...16
        4. Service..17
        5. Volley: Forehand and Backhand Volley 19
        6. Drop Volley 20
        7. Half Volley 21
        8. Lob..21
        9. Overhead Smash 21
        10. Return of Serve 22
        11. Advanced Variations for Groundstrokes........................22
    C. Strategy 23
    D. Court Conduct..27
    E. Rules 28
    F. Scoring 29

Chapter Three
Exercises
    A. Flexibility..31
    B. Strength 32
    C. Cardiovascular Fitness 32

Chapter Four
Drills 33

Chapter Five
Sample Lesson Plans
- Lesson One: Background Material. 37
- Lesson Two: Forehand. 38
- Lesson Three: Forehand. 39
- Lesson Four: Backhand. 39
- Lesson Five: Backhand. 39
- Lesson Six: Service. 40
- Lesson Seven: Rules & Scoring. 40
- Lesson Eight: Court Position and Conduct. 41
- Lesson Nine: Game Workshops. 41
- Lesson Ten: Game Workshops. 41
- Lesson Eleven: Multiple Skill Levels 42

Chapter Six
Evaluation
- A. Program Evaluation 43
- B. Player Evaluation 43
  - 1. Psychomotor 43
    - a) Stroke Evaluation 43
    - b) Visual Assessment 43
  - 2. Cognitive 44
  - 3. Affective 44

Appendix I   Reference Materials 45
- A. Books 45
- B. Periodicals 45
- C. Films 45
- D. Tennis Associations 45

Appendix II   Equipment 45

Appendix III CTA Examiner's Test Sheet 46
              CTA Levels Tests 46

Chapter One
Format And Purpose Of The Handbook

A. Introduction

In this handbook ideas are presented on the teaching of racquet sports by way of objectives, program content, teaching methods, sample lesson plans, and evaluation. The handbook emphasizes the psychomotor aspects of skill development but does not negate the very important aspects of knowledge and attitude in tennis.

Interest in tennis as a leisure time activity has increased tremendously over the last few years. The biggest development is an attempt at Canada-wide standardization of instruction. The Canadian Tennis Association has outlined specific levels for teaching the various tennis skills. The idea is that a player should be able to move from one type of instruction to another and still cover the basic tennis skills.

For this reason we have followed the CTA levels guidelines so that a player may move from the school program to the recreation or club program without missing or repeating material. In the long run this will upgrade the level of tennis in Canada. (See Appendix for listings of Canadian and American Tennis Associations.)

B. Purpose of the Handbook

This handbook is an extension of the Physical Education Curriculum and Resource Guide (1980).
The information included in the handbook is designed to provide the instructor with a comprehensive source of information for teaching Tennis.

C. Handbook Format

The handbook describes in detail the skills required for playing Tennis and the recommended techniques for teaching them, suggests drills which can be used to practice these skills, offers sample lesson plans for the use of the instructor, and discusses methods of evaluation. The guidelines presented in this handbook are suggestions only and may be adapted as the instructor becomes more familiar with Tennis.

D. Objectives of the Program

Tennis is a "lifetime" sport. Due to the nature of the game it can be played and enjoyed by people of all ages and levels of proficiency. Public courts and the limited, relatively inexpensive equipment necessary, put the game within the reach of almost everyone. Tennis offers a healthy way to relieve the tensions of everyday living and is a "fun" way to become physically active and to enjoy one's leisure time. There are three major objectives to the tennis program:

1. Psychomotor Objectives

a) Players should be able to perform the basic skills to such a degree that they can be used in a game situation.
b) Players should improve fitness through participation in the warm-up exercises, skill development drills, and game situations.

2. Cognitive Objectives

a) Players should be able to keep score and follow the game rules and rules of court etiquette in a game situation.
b) Players should be able to analyze their strokes and if necessary make the appropriate corrections.

3. Affective Objectives

a) Players should demonstrate a positive attitude toward the game by cooperating in practice and game situations.
b) Players should be able to appreciate the physical and mental benefits that tennis provides.

E. Application To Classroom Teaching

1. Tennis Facilities

The most appropriate and ideal learning environment would be a tennis court complex composed of two or three courts and a ten-meter long practice wall enclosed by a chain link fence.

This facility is desirable but not essential. Skills could be developed in a gymnasium with rules, scoring, and a game strategy introduced in a classroom setting. Some court time would be advisable to allow students to develop judgment and control. If the school does not have tennis courts some arrangements could be made to use public facilities during non-prime times.

2. Teaching Strategy

The Canadian Tennis Association subscribes to a set of teaching strategies or guidelines which would be very appropriate to this program and its integration into the classroom or community center. These are:

a) Teach confidence and a positive attitude, that is, positive reinforcement.

b) Teach progressively from simple to more complex skills.
c) Teach the whole action first, only breaking it down to partial motions if necessary.
d) Teach percentage tennis, that is, steadiness, depth, accuracy, power.
e) Teach actions corresponding to actual playing conditions.
f) Teach practice with a purpose.
g) Teach by short verbal explanations followed by precise demonstration.
h) Group lessons require concise planning.

A prime consideration in developing a teaching strategy is to encourage a positive attitude toward tennis. The instructional program must be an enjoyable learning experience. Playing tennis has to be self-motivating to encourage extra-curricular participation. The initial exposure must be fun while at the same time providing basic skills and a healthy attitude toward recreational or competitive tennis.

There are four psychological considerations which can aid in effective instruction:

1. **Positive reinforcement:** Focus on good points of the player's abilities.
2. **A relaxed atmosphere:** Tennis strokes emanate from relaxed movements, so instructor goals for player success must be easily attainable by each participant.
3. **Feedback:** Player skill problems must be corrected by positively reinforcing the good points while drawing attention to the problems.
4. **Recognition of recreational or competitive tendencies:** These attributes should have outlets to provide for further development of skills through participation.

Success is certainly the prime motivation among players. The degree of success is determined by level of skill development and attitude. If a player is made to "feel good" about whatever level of skill is attained, then continued participation can only heighten the skill level.

F. Description of Levels Approach

The "levels system" refers to a sequentially developed program of activities, focusing on psychomotor skills, cognitive skills and affective skills with particular emphasis on psychomotor skills.
Tennis instruction should begin with simple activities and progress to the more complex. However, progression is dependent on the individual player rather than being determined by any grade level. The levels approach, explained later in this chapter, has been developed to reinforce this concept.

The four-level system is as follows:

HANDBOOK DESIGNATION	CANADIAN TENNIS ASSOCIATION DESIGNATION
Level I	- Beginner
Level II	- Novice
Level III	- Intermediate
Level IV	- Tournament (Advanced)

Since most tennis players learn the game through recreational, club or school programs, standardization of the levels progression system is important. This will allow players to transfer from one program to another with ease. Individuals can participate in school lessons and then further their abilities in recreational programs without repeating or missing material.

Each level serves as a stage to introduce and develop some of the necessary skills. The next level reinforces existing skills and adds new material. This process allows accent on the basic tennis skills while developing an extensive repertoire of strokes.

The activity sequence chart describes the skills which are to be taught and developed at each of the four levels. It also outlines some exercises and drills that will be invaluable to the teacher.

Level IV, the advanced or tournament level, may be subdivided into competitive and recreational categories. This is important, so that players can realize personal goals in either of these areas.

G. Explanation Of The Activity Sequence Chart

The activity sequence chart outlines the basic skills required when playing tennis and includes useful drills and exercises.

The strokes in the chart have been described for right-handed players. Instructors and coaches should remember to make the necessary changes to accommodate left-handed players who may have a psychological block when trying to learn the game. Often these players feel that everything is harder because they are left-handed. Instructors can offer encouragement by pointing out that some of the best players in the world have been left-handers. Most right-handed players find it much harder to play against a left-hander because they have to change their tactics. The video tapes outlined in Appendix I do an excellent job of demonstrating the strokes for right and left-handed players.

The activity sequence chart is designed as a reference for instructors and should not be used as a lesson plan. When instructing tennis remember the basic teaching strategies. Keep it simple!

H. Activity Sequence Chart

SKILLS	I	II	III	IV
A. Basic Skills				
1. Ball Control and Racquet Skills				
a) watching the ball	•			
b) grips	•			
i eastern forehand	•			
ii eastern backhand	•			
iii continental	•			
c) hand-eye coordination	•			
d) racquet faces	•			
2. Footwork				
a) balance	•			
b) weight transfer	•			
c) ready position	•			
3. Ball Pick-up	•			
B. Individual Skills				
1. Forehand Groundstroke				
a) grip	•			
b) stroke components				
i ready position	•			
ii preparation	•			
iii impact	•			
iv follow-through	•			
2. Backhand Groundstroke				
a) grip	•			
b) stroke components	•			
i ready position	•			
ii preparation	•			
iii impact	•			
iv follow through	•			
c) backhand variations				
i semi-two-handed backhand	•			
ii two-handed backhand	•			
3. Service				
a) grip	•			
b) stroke components				
i ready position	•			
ii ball toss	•			
iii preparation	•			
iv impact	•			
v follow-through	•			
4. Volley (forehand and backhand)				
a) grip		•		
i ready position		•		
ii preparation		•		

SKILLS	I	II	III	IV
iii impact		•		
iv follow-through		•		
5. Drop Volley			•	
6. Half Volley			•	
7. Lob			•	
8. Overhead Smash			•	
9. Return of Serve		•		
10. Advanced Variations for Groundstroke				
a) no spin				•
b) topspin				•
c) backspin				•
d) sidespin				•
C. Strategy				
1. Beginners				
a) singles		•		
b) doubles		•		
2. Advanced				
a) singles				•
b) doubles				•
D. Court Conduct	•			
E. Rules	•			
F. Scoring	•			

I. Relationship of Tennis to Goals and Learning Outcomes

A major goal and learning outcome of the program is to promote physical fitness for a lifetime. Tennis hopes to offer an activity that players will enjoy enough to play outside of school or commercial recreation time and in their adult years. If the basic objectives are achieved, then the major goal and learning outcome will also be achieved. People will play tennis more often which will increase their physical activity and as a result improve their fitness level.

Chapter Two
Skill Development and Teaching Techniques

A. Basic Skills

SKILL	DESCRIPTION	TEACHING TECHNIQUES AND OBSERVATION POINTS
1. Ball Control and Racquet Skills	These are basic to good tennis. Before a player begins to try to stroke the ball over the net, there are some fundamentals that must be mastered.	1. Emphasize that if players can develop the following skills the rest of the game will be much easier to learn. 2. To avoid confusion for left and right-handed players, the terms racquet hand and non-racquet hand can be used.
a) Watching the ball	Every player should watch the ball from the moment it leaves the opponent's racquet to the moment it comes in contact with their racquet.	1. **Watching the ball is the most important skill in tennis.** 2. This must not be taken for granted: it is a skill that requires practice 3. Seventy percent of all errors result from taking the eye off the ball prior to contact. 4. Concentrated watching of the ball gives the player better judgment of the speed and bounce of the oncoming ball. 5. No matter what skill is being taught, emphasize "watching the ball."
b) Grips	The grip must suit the shot.	1. The way a player holds the racquet affects the angle of the face of the racquet. 2. There are different grips for forehand, backhand, service, and volley.
i Eastern Forehand Grip 	The Eastern forehand grip is commonly known as the "shake hands" grip. This grip is used to play forehand groundstrokes. 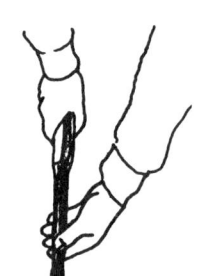 **Common Error**	1. Hold the racquet at the throat with the non-racquet hand (left) so that the face of the racquet is perpendicular to the ground. 2. "Shake hands" with the racquet so that the "V" formed by the thumb and index finger are on the sides of the racquet. 3. Hold the racquet as close to the butt as is comfortably possible while still feeling control of the head of the racquet. 4. Grip must be firm so that the impact of the ball will not twist the racquet, but not so tight that there is no feeling of "touch" on striking the ball. A normal firm handshake is a good guide to the right amount of pressure. Watch for players who have fingers spread too far apart, or hold the racquet like a hammer. Practice "shaking hands."

SKILL	DESCRIPTION	TEACHING TECHNIQUES AND OBSERVATION POINTS
ii Eastern Backhand Grip 	The Eastern backhand grip is a modified forehand grip. The grip is changed to adjust the angle of the face of the racquet for backhand groundstrokes.	1. Racquet is held at the throat with the left hand. The right hand is holding the grip with a loose Eastern forehand grip. 2. To change to a backhand grip turn racquet one quarter turn to the right. 3. "V" formed by the thumb and index finger is on the left edge of the grip of the racquet. 5. Thumb is placed across the handle. 6. Players should practice switching from the forehand to the backhand grip so that the change becomes automatic. 7. Emphasize using the left hand to turn the racquet so that a proper firm grip may be formed.
iii Continental 	This is the best grip for the serve and volley and is a comfortable grip between the forehand and the backhand grips.	1. Racquet is held at the throat by the left hand. Right hand is in a loose Eastern forehand grip. 2. To change to the Continental grip turn racquet one eighth turn to the right. 3. "V" formed by the thumb and index finger is on the left edge of the racquet. (Similar to backhand but slightly closer to forehand.) 4. Thumb is around the handle, instead of across as it is in the backhand grip. 5. Allow players to make little adjustments for the sake of comfort.
c) Hand-eye Coordination	Hand and eye coordination in tennis is often called ball sense. Ball sense is judgment of what a tennis ball may do when it is hit and when it bounces. Ball sense is a learned skill and can be developed through the use of drills. **Ball sense drills** 1. Without a racquet  a) Throwing and Catching b) Bouncing and Catching	1. Ball sense can be improved by playing, or simply hitting and catching a ball. 2. Key to all ball sense drills is - "Watch the ball." 3. The better a player becomes at the ball sense drills, the easier it is to learn the basic strokes. 1. With racquet hand, throw the ball into the air and catch it. 2. "Watch the ball" right into the hand. Concentrate; try to see how the ball spins. 1. With racquet hand, bounce ball to the ground or rebound ball from a wall to the ground and then catch it. 2. Again, "watch the ball" right into the hand. Look for the various ways the ball spins. The above drills can be modified so player may work with a partner. Another variation is to work with more than one ball.

SKILL	DESCRIPTION	TEACHING TECHNIQUES AND OBSERVATION POINTS
	2. With a racquet	
	Doing the ball sense drills with a racquet gets the player used to holding the racquet properly and also developing forearm strength.	1. When doing ball sense drills with a racquet, always concentrate on correct grip and firm wrist. 2. Again, emphasize "watching the ball."
	Bouncing ball on racquet 	1. With forehand grip bounce the ball up and down on the strings of the racquet. Try to do this 100 times consecutively. Make sure wrist is firm - "watch the ball." 2. To develop control, try to increase the number of consecutive hits. Have contests to see how many hits can be made in two minutes.
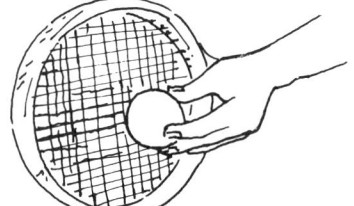	Bouncing ball from racquet to the ground.	1. With the forehand grip and a firm wrist, bounce the ball to the ground. 2. This can be done while the player walks or runs around a court. NOTE: 1. A tightness in the forearm muscle should be felt after practicing the drill. This indicates that the forearm is being strengthened. 2. These drills can be used as relays and contests to motivate players to practice and work hard (see "Wimbledon Relays" p. 33).
d) Racquet Faces	The racquet face is the hitting platform formed by the strings of the racquet. The angle of the face of the racquet is determined by wrist control. There are three basic racquet faces	Angle of the racquet face puts spin on the tennis ball. This is sometimes done deliberately but most often for beginners it is accidental.
	i Neutral or Flat	1. Racquet face is perpendicular to the ground. 2. Racquet is an extension of the arm with the wrist firm and straight. 3. Hitting the ball with a flat face will put little or no spin on the ball. 4. Beginners should concentrate on hitting groundstrokes with a flat or neutral face.
	ii Open	1. Racquet face is tilted slightly upward. 2. This is caused by the hand and wrist turning slightly under the racquet. 3. When done deliberately by advanced players this will put backspin on the ball. 4. When done accidentally it will cause the ball to go very high and usually long. 5. To correct -- emphasize keeping the wrist firm. This can be done by strengthening the wrist.

SKILL	DESCRIPTION	TEACHING TECHNIQUES AND OBSERVATION POINTS
iii Closed 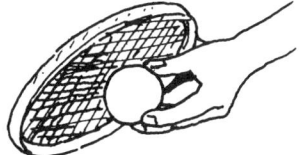		1. Racquet face tilts slightly toward the ground. 2. This is caused by the hand and wrist turning slightly over the racquet. 3. When done deliberately this will put topspin on the ball. 4. When done accidentally it causes the ball to be hit into the net or to fall shallow in the opponent's court. 5. The correction is the same as for an open face.
2. Footwork	Correct footwork is possibly the most common weakness in tennis players above the elementary or beginner level. Poor footwork leads to poor positioning. Only from a good position can players hit good strokes consistently.	1. Tennis running requires quick and unexpected stops and changes in direction and speed. 2. The center of gravity should be kept low and when running, the steps should be shorter. 3. The basic principle in tennis running is to get sideways into a striking position. 4. It is important for players to remember to return to the basic court position (one or two steps behind the center of the baseline) immediately after completing the stroke. 5. Good footwork allows fluent transition from stroke to stroke.

a) Balance	Balance and footwork are highly dependent upon each other. Poor footwork leads to discomfort when stroking and this discomfort often leads to loss of balance. The opposite is also true: poor balance leads to poor footwork as no one can get off the mark quickly or move well unless properly balanced. Balance on impact is essential to allow the best chance of aiming and controlling the ball.	1. The basis of good balance is the ready position and the return to that position in preparation for the next shot.
		2. Poor balance forces a player to compensate when hitting the ball. For example,
		  a) Large rushed steps
		  b) Lunges toward the ball
		  c) Excessive use of the wrist.

b) Weight Transfer Control	In order to play economically but with good power and precision, a good player must learn how to transfer weight forward at impact.	1. Weight transfer takes strain off the arm. By transferring the weight at impact, speed and accuracy of the shot is increased. 2. Good balance and footwork are fundamental to good weight transfer. 3. At the moment of the impact the weight should shift from the back foot to the front foot. 4. Whenever a stroke is finished with body weight on the back foot, the shot was played "out of balance." 5. Players should practice this weight transfer by "shadowing" the various strokes.

SKILL	DESCRIPTION	TEACHING TECHNIQUES AND OBSERVATION POINTS
c) Ready Position	The ready position is the basic or neutral position from which to begin to excute a stroke and to which the player returns after completing the stroke. The ball is ready to be played.	1. Feet should be shoulder-width apart. 2. Knees are bent and flexible. 3. Upper body is kept straight with the weight on the toes. 4. Racquet is held in front of the body with both hands, right hand on handle, left hand supporting racquet at the throat. 5. Elbows should be bent and kept close to the body. 6. Head of racquet should be kept above the wrist. 7. Player should be relaxed but alert, and ready to go

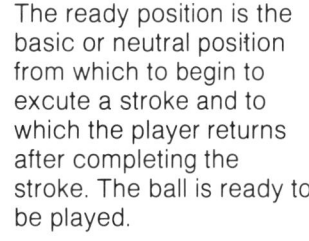

Ready Position

3. Ball Pick-up

	This is one skill that all players must master. Especially at the beginner stage, much of the time on the court is spent picking up tennis balls.	1. Place left foot close to ball. 2. Trap ball between instep and the tip of the racquet. 3. Gently lift racquet and foot at the same time. Ball is lifted into the air. 4. Bounce ball with the racquet and catch it.

Trap   Lift   Bounce

B. Individual Skills

1. Forehand Groundstroke

This is one of the basic tennis strokes. It is used to hit the ball after it has bounced on the player's right (racquet) side.

a) Grip - Eastern Forehand

Eastern forehand or "shake hands" grip. Described under Ball Control and Racquet Skills.

SKILL	DESCRIPTION	TEACHING TECHNIQUES AND OBSERVATION POINTS
b) Stroke Components	**i** Ready position -- Player is poised, waiting, ready to hit the ball.	See Ready Position under Footwork. |айн

SKILL	DESCRIPTION	TEACHING TECHNIQUES AND OBSERVATION POINTS

b) Stroke Components

i Ready position -- Player is poised, waiting, ready to hit the ball.

See Ready Position under Footwork.

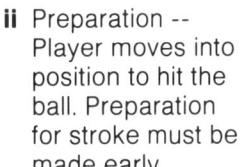

ii Preparation -- Player moves into position to hit the ball. Preparation for stroke must be made early.

1. From ready position, pivot on right foot to get to a position sideways to the net.
2. As player pivots the racquet should start its backswing.
3. Backswing should always be lower than the level of the oncoming ball and never higher than the level of the shoulders.
4. Racquet should be brought back with the elbow bent and close to the body.
5. Racquet is supported with left hand until forearm is parallel to the net.
6. Knees are bent with weight on the right foot.

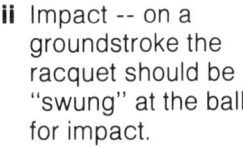

iii Impact -- on a groundstroke the racquet should be "swung" at the ball for impact.

The most important rule is "watch the ball."

1. The weight is shifted forward by stepping onto the left foot as racquet begins its forward swing.
2. When starting the forward swing, the head of the racquet should be below the level of the oncoming ball, but above the level of the wrist.
3. Wrist is kept firm throughout the entire stroke.
4. Knees are bent a little less than during the preparation.
5. Left arm comes across to assist balance.
6. Arm stays slightly bent until moment of impact.
7. Ball is contacted in front of the left hip with a slightly rising swing.
8. Weight is on the left foot, the right foot stays on the ground for balance.

SKILL	DESCRIPTION	TEACHING TECHNIQUES AND OBSERVATION POINTS
	iv Follow-through -- racquet should always end up higher than it was at the moment of impact.	1. After impact, racquet follows through along with the right shoulder. 2. Left arm assists in balance and shoulder rotation. 3. Racquet gradually rises as knees straighten to the level of ready position. 4. Racquet finishes edgeways to the ground and in front of left shoulder. 5. Remember, racquet is always higher than it was at the moment of impact.
2. Backhand Groundstroke	The backhand groundstroke is another basic tennis stroke used to hit the ball after it has bounced on the player's non-racquet side.	
a) Grip	Eastern backhand	See Eastern Backhand Grip under Ball Control and Racquet Skills.
b) Stroke Components	 i Ready position - same position as forehand. Player is poised to see where the opponent is going to hit the ball. Grip should be changed to ready position.	
	ii Preparation - remember to make the preparation early.	1. From ready position player pivots on left foot to a position sideways to the net. Right shoulder is forward and at an angle slightly more than perpendicular to the net. 2. At the same time as the player is getting into the sideways position the racquet should begin its backswing. 3. Backswing should always be lower than the level of the ball and never higher than the shoulders. 4. Racquet should be brought back with the elbow bent and close to the body.

SKILL	DESCRIPTION	TEACHING TECHNIQUES AND OBSERVATION POINTS

5. The left hand pulls the throat of the racquet back and supports the racquet while waiting for impact.
6. Knees are bent and weight is on the left foot.

iii Impact

1. Weight is shifted forward by stepping onto right foot as racquet begins its forward swing.
2. When starting forward swing, head of racquet should be below the oncoming ball, but above the level of the wrist.
3. Wrist is kept firm throughout the entire stroke.
4. Knees are bent less than during preparation.
5. Arm stays slightly bent until the moment of impact.
6. Ball is contacted in front of the right hip, with a slightly rising swing.
7. Weight is on right foot; left foot remains on the ground for balance.

iv Follow-through

1. After impact, racquet continues its forward motion and player finishes up with the knees straightening to the level of ready position.
2. At the end of follow-through, arm is extended.
3. Racquet is high in front of left shoulder, higher than at the moment of impact.
4. Shoulders remain perpendicular to net.

c) Backhand Variations

Several successful players have emerged in recent years with a punishing two-handed backstroke. This has lead to some variations to the backhand groundstroke.

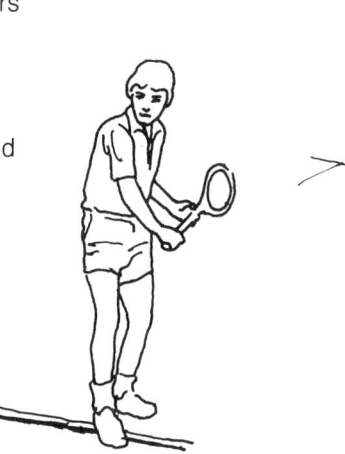

i Semi-two-handed backhand: Left hand guides and steadies the throat to the impact.

1. All basic rules for a backhand hit apply to a semi-two-handed backhand except that the backswing is shorter.
2. The major difference is the use of the left hand.
3. Left hand guides and steadies the racquet throat pushing it until just after the impact point.

SKILL	DESCRIPTION	TEACHING TECHNIQUES AND OBSERVATION POINTS
	ii Two-handed backhand: The left hand stays on racquet for entire stroke.	1. Right hand should dominate the stroke. 2. Right hand grips racquet with backhand grip. Left hand takes a supporting position above and behind the right hand. 3. Backswing for a two-handed backhand is shorter. 4. Both hands remain on racquet for entire stroke, including follow-through.
	Advantages of the semi-two-handed and the two-handed backhand.	1. Help make up for weak wrist. 2. Shots are difficult to "read." 3. More precision. 4. Makes shoulders turn automatically. 5. Shorter backswings make strokes more efficient.
	Disadvantages of the semi-two-handed and the two-handed backhand.	1. Reach is restricted and as a result requires player to get closer to the ball in order to be in correct hitting position. 2. Poses balance problems. 3. Uncomfortable for volleying because of balance problems and lack of reach.
3. Forehand and Backhand: Common Errors and Stroke Correction	When correcting strokes emphasize "Watching the ball."	This is the most important skill in tennis.
	Common Faults	
	i Insufficient rotation of shoulder	Concentrate on turning more.
	ii Backswing too high	Hold throat of racquet with left hand as long as possible during preparation.
	iii Dropping head of the racquet	1. Hold throat of racquet with left hand. 2. Keep wrist firm.
	iv Elbow too far from body	1. Turn sideways more. 2. Try to hit ball without dropping another ball that has been tucked under the armpit.
	v Arm too straight	1. Concentrate on hitting ball while elbow is bent. 2. Move a little closer to ball.
	vi Follow-through too short	1. Imagine that the racquet is pointing at the spot where the ball has been hit. 2. On the forehand, try to take the throat of racquet with the left hand high in front of the left shoulder at the end of the motion.

SKILL	DESCRIPTION	TEACHING TECHNIQUES AND OBSERVATION POINTS
	vii Stepping forward with right foot before hitting ball	1. Do not try to hit too hard. 2. Make sure that point of impact is not too far in front of the body. 3. Concentrate on keeping back foot in place through entire motion.
	viii Tendency to hit too hard	1. Concentrate on keeping balls in court. 2. Aim to hit balls about one and one half meters above net.
	ix Using too much wrist	1. Do not try for additional speed with wrist action. 2. Keep wrist firm. 3. Hit easily and develop control.
4. Service	The serve is one of the most important strokes in tennis. Beginners should try to develop a good *first* and *second* serve.	1. A good server will get the first serve eighty percent of the time. 2. Many people feel that "a player is only as good as his or her second serve." Keep it in the court and deep.
	When learning the serve remember that it is the only stroke in the game with which time can be taken. Take advantage of this rule.	1. Concentrate before starting service motion. 2. Do not rush the motion. 3. If toss is poor, *do not hit it*. Players are allowed to re-toss the ball until satisfied with the toss.
a) Grip	Continental	See Continental Grip under Ball Control and Racquet Skills.
b) Stroke Components	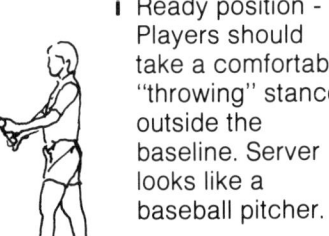 **i** Ready position - Players should take a comfortable "throwing" stance outside the baseline. Server looks like a baseball pitcher.	1. Left foot is at a forty-five degree angle toward the baseline and three to five centimeters behind it. 2. Right foot is shoulder-width distance behind the left. 3. Racquet is held by right hand in the Continental grip. Left hand supports throat of racquet. 4. Weight should be evenly distributed. 5. Relax!
	 **ii** Preparation - motion begins with both arms starting their different actions simultaneously. This action is often referred to as the "scissor" motion.	1. As left arm is raised to "place" ball into the air, the racquet is swung down and back into the "backscratch" position. 2. Racquet swings down past right leg and up behind the back with elbow bent, wrist relaxed, and head of the racquet dropped between the shoulders. This is the "backscratch" position. 3. Weight shifts onto back foot. 4. After ball is "placed" in the air, left hand remains pointing at ball. This helps the balance and timing of the swing.

SKILL	DESCRIPTION	TEACHING TECHNIQUES AND OBSERVATION POINTS
	**iii** Ball toss - the most difficult part of the serve. Players should practice until it becomes consistently accurate. Remember: If toss is poor do not try to hit it. Ball may be retossed until it is in the right position.	1. Ball is tossed from fingertips of left (non-racquet) hand. 2. Arm lifts and ball is "placed" into the air with relatively straight arm. 3. Ball should be "placed" into the air a racquet's length into the court and about fifteen to twenty-five centimeters higher than can be reached with the racquet. 4. Take time to place the ball gently into the air. Don't throw it.
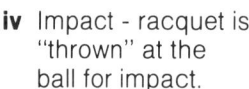	**iv** Impact - racquet is "thrown" at the ball for impact. "Watch the ball"	1. From the "backscratch" position the racquet is thrown up and forward to hitting position. 2. Throwing motion is achieved by moving elbow forward and upward at the same time as the wrist snaps the head of the racquet from the "backscratch" position. This should be controlled motion. 3. Impact point is at the comfortable maximum height of reach, a little to the right of the head and just in front of the body. 4. At moment of impact, the right arm, body and racquet are at full extension. 5. Shoulders are parallel to the net. 6. Left arm keeps the balance. 7. Weight has shifted onto front foot.
	**v** Follow-through - the follow-through should be very pronounced. Imagine throwing the racquet out and over the net.	1. Head of racquet follows flight line of ball as long as comfortably possible. 2. Racquet swings out and then downward across the body, ending on left side. 3. Left foot is holding all weight as the right foot is naturally pulled forward for balance. 4. Player may step into court after racquet has contacted ball.
c) Common Errors and Stroke Correction	**i** Trying to hit ball too hard	1. This is the most common mistake that beginners make when learning the serve. 2. Emphasize control rather than speed.
	ii Tossing the ball too low and behind the body	1. Measure correct height of toss near the court fence or near some permanent fixture. 2. Practice keeping ball-tossing arm well extended in front of body. 3. A correctly tossed ball should drop about forty-five centimeters in front of the left foot.

SKILL	DESCRIPTION	TEACHING TECHNIQUES AND OBSERVATION POINTS
	iii Moving left foot and stepping forward with right foot before hitting ball.	1. Concentrate on keeping both feet on the ground in unchanged position through entire motion. 2. Make sure contact point is not too far in front of the body.
	iv Incorrect grip resulting in hitting the ball too flatly without any spin or control.	1. Use Continental grip. 2. Imagine throwing edge of racquet at ball.
	v Hitting ball while elbow is bent.	1. This is due to poor timing and poor coordination caused either by a low toss or by waiting too long. 2. Do not try to hit a poorly tossed ball. 3. Always try to reach for tossed ball and hit it at its peak.
	vi Not dropping racquet head low enough behind body.	1. Bend elbow properly. 2. Keep wrist loose behind the body.
	vii Pushing racquet instead of throwing it at ball.	1. Practice throwing ball over net with racquet hand. 2. Now grip the racquet and pretend to throw it over net. 3. Both motions should feel the same.
5. Forehand and Backhand Volley	A volley is the stroke used to hit the ball before it bounces. The strokes are so similar in both forehand and backhand that they will be described together.	1. The backhand is the most suitable net-stroke for the fastest reflex action in the game. 2. Players should know that the backhand is the easiest and handiest stroke for volleying balls coming towards the body.
a) Grip	Because the volley is so fast, there is little preparation time with this stroke. The Continental grip is best for the volley since it can be used for both forehand and backhand volley.	See Continental Grip under Ball Control and Racquet Skills.

b) Stroke Components 	**i** Ready position - similar to the ready position for groundstrokes. The volley position on the court is two to three meters away from the net.	1. See Ready Position under Footwork.
		2. There are a few slight differences from the groundstroke ready position.
		   a) Grip is the Continental grip.
		   b) Feet are a little wider apart.
		   c) Back is bent slightly forward.
		   d) Arms are loosely bent in front of the body with head of racquet higher.

SKILL	DESCRIPTION	TEACHING TECHNIQUES AND OBSERVATION POINTS
	**ii** Preparation	1. Pivot on back foot and turn shoulders so that line of shoulders is diagonal to the net (forty-five degrees). 2. Keeping head of the racquet up, take it back to a position parallel to the net.
	iii Impact "Watch the ball"	1. Firm wrist is the key to successful volleying. 2. Block or punch through the ball with a locked wrist and a shade of backspin for better control (see Spins p. 22) 3. Hit ball well in front of the body with a straight arm. 4. Keep elbow close to the body, except for high volleys when the ball is hit more in front of the body. 5. For low volleys, open the face of the racquet a little more, keep it in a horizontal position. 6. Weight shifts onto front foot as player steps toward ball at impact.
	iv Follow-through	1. The volley is a short, crisp punch. 2. There should be little or no follow-through, unless a volley is made on an easy ball when more follow-through is used to push the ball away.
c) Common Errors and Stroke Corrections	**i** Backswing too long	1. Stand against a wall and have a partner throw some balls to volley. 2. The wall will stop the backswing from going behind the body.
	ii Racquet head too low	1. Keep racquet head higher in ready position. 2. Imagine saluting with the head of the racquet when volleying.
	iii Hitting the ball beside behind the body	Go to the net without a racquet and have players practice catching the ball well in front of the body with the racquet hand.
	iv Loose wrist	1. Concentrate on keeping wrist firm and rigid with head of racquet up. 2. Do not try to hit by swinging - block the ball as it comes.
6. Drop Volley	Drop volley is commonly known as a stop volley. The ball is deflected over the net at a shallow angle so that it has a very shallow bounce.	1. Stroke is exactly the same as a regular volley except for impact and follow-through. 2. At impact the racquet will "give" to counteract the force of the ball. 3. Ball should be hit with backspin so that it does not bounce very high. 4. Follow-through is slightly downward. 5. The drop volley is considered a touch shot. It requires practice and timing.

SKILL	DESCRIPTION	TEACHING TECHNIQUES AND OBSERVATION POINTS
7. Half Volley	Half volley is technically a groundstroke. Ball is hit a split second after it bounces. It is a very difficult stroke to hit because it is very difficult to judge and time.	1. Motion used for a half volley is the same as for a regular volley. 2. Ball is blocked, so there is little backswing or follow-through. 3. Racquet face should be slightly closed. 4. Players should avoid the half volley where possible. The half volley is purely a defensive stroke and usually a result of poor anticipation or court positioning. 5. Try to move up and take the ball on the volley or move back and hit the groundstroke.
8. Lob	A lob is any ball that is lofted high into the air, usually over the head of an opponent. The lob is one of the most underestimated strokes in the modern game. Deception and depth are two keys to a good lob.	1. The lob should be hit with the same motion as forehand or backhand groundstrokes but with a very short backswing and a long, full, lifting follow-through. 2. Face of racquet should be slightly open. 3. To get more control, many players hit the lob with a little backspin.

9. Overhead Smash	Overhead smash is an offensive stroke. Ball is taken high over the head and smashed down. It is used against a lob or very high bouncing ball. The motion of the overhead is very similar to that of the serve.	
a) Grip	Continental grip	
b) Stroke Components	**i** Ready Position	

SKILL	DESCRIPTION	TEACHING TECHNIQUES AND OBSERVATION POINTS
	ii Preparation	1. Turn sideways to the net (service ready position). 2. Point left hand toward ball for timing. 3. Racquet is moved into the "backscratch" position ready to hit the ball. 4. Get set under the flight line of the ball.
	iii Impact "Watch the ball"	1. "Throw" racquet head at ball while stepping forward in the direction of the shot. 2. Hit hard and flat.
	iv Follow-through	Shorter than for the serve; get back to ready position quickly. When teaching the overhead to beginners emphasize the similarity to the serve.
10. Return of Serve	Return of serve is considered by many to be the most important stroke in the game. Players at the recreational level lose forty percent of the points because the serve is not returned into play.	1. The number one rule on return of serve is "Get the Ball Back." 2. Use a very short backswing and follow-through when returning a hard serve. Ball should be blocked with a "volley" type of stroke. 3. Never try to hit too many winners on a return of serve. 4. If server misses first serve move in one or two steps because second serve is generally slower. Moving in also puts psychological pressure on server. 5. "Watch the ball."
11. Advanced Variations for Ground-strokes-spins	Spin can play an important part in several strokes. It affects the flight and bounce of the ball. Types of hits:	Level IV or advanced players sometimes use spin on groundstrokes to vary shots.
	a) Flat -- no spin	1. Beginners should learn to hit good, flat groundstrokes before spins are attempted. 2. Flat stroke is obtained by hitting the ball straight on with a perfectly flat racquet face. 3. Ball has little or no spin and as a result has the highest speed. 4. A ball without spin also has a "normal" trajectory and a regular bounce.

SKILL	DESCRIPTION	TEACHING TECHNIQUES AND OBSERVATION POINTS
	b) Topspin	1. Topspin is obtained with a slightly closed racquet face. 2. Hit from slightly behind and below the ball, then the stroke continues up and through the ball. 3. Ball hit with topspin has a shorter trajectory. 4. Speed of the ball after it bounces is faster than it is before it bounces. This makes the ball harder to judge. 5. Topspin tends to make the ball bounce higher.
	c) Backspin	1. The reverse of topspin. 2. Backspin is obtained with a slightly open racquet face. 3. Hit from slightly above and behind the ball, then the stroke continues down and through the ball. 4. Backspin causes the ball to float longer in the court. 5. When ball bounces it loses much of its forward momentum. This tends to make the ball slide and have a low bounce.
	d) Sidespin	1. Sidespin is the least used spin. 2. Ball is caused to spin on its vertical axis. 3. Sidespin is obtained by drawing racquet across the ball toward the body. 4. When ball bounces it tends to slide in the direction of the spin.

C. Strategy

1. Beginners

a) Singles	Games should be permitted as soon as a reasonable amount of shot control has been developed. At this level the key word is "simplicity." The simplest plan at this level is to try to outrally (outsteady) one's opponent. A steady game should be the objective and is the winning way for beginners. The player who makes the fewest mistakes wins. Errors lose tennis matches far more often than brilliant shots win them. "Keep the ball in play" and learn to play percentage tennis right from the beginning.	1. Beginners should be aware that cross-court shots are tactically easier to play than down-the-line shots. Cross-courts have the longest possible trajectory and because the height of the net is lowest in the middle where the ball must pass over, there is more margin for error. 2. Remember that seventy-five percent of errors are balls in the net, only twenty-five percent are out balls.
	i Strategy - Until now, major emphasis has been on how the	1. Good court positioning is essential. The player should start about one meter behind the baseline approximately in the middle of the court. (5) 2. Numbers show where to stand in a game of singles for

SKILL	DESCRIPTION	TEACHING TECHNIQUES AND OBSERVATION POINTS

	ball should be hit. Strategy deals with where to hit the ball and when to hit it there.	specific shots.
		  1. Serving into the forehand court.
		  2. Serving into the backhand court.
		  3. Receiving a serve on the forehand side of the court.
		  4. Receiving a serve on the backhand side of the court.
		  5. Playing during a rally.
		  6. Playing for volleying at net.
		3. Avoid getting caught in "no man's land." It is the worst place on the court from which to return an opponent's shot.

	Strategy is really nothing more than developing a game plan. Such a plan should be based upon a complete and objective analysis of the following:	1. One's own game. 2. One's opponent's game. 3. The environmental conditions (court surface, weather, balls and so on).
	ii Tactics - Tactics covers the implementation of one's game plan in a match. The most important points for implementing the proper tactics are:	1. Decide how and where to hit before starting the backswing. 2. Use a variety of strokes, mix speed, spin and placements. 3. Concentrate and keep self-control under all circumstances. 4. Learn to play percentage shots: force one's opponent to make errors while minimizing one's own. 5. Learn to anticipate the right position on the court. 6. Be aware of key points and try extra hard to win them. 7. Be adaptable. Do not change a winning game, but always be ready to change a losing one.

b) Doubles	The most important difference between singles and doubles is the way the player must think. Teamwork and a "forgive and forget" nature win more doubles matches than individual brilliance.
	
	The basic secret of a good doubles team is to have two people who feel comfortable together and who enjoy being a team even when the going gets tough.
		1. Two key features of any doubles game are teamwork and offense.
		2. Proper court position is the most important factor in successful doubles at the beginner level. The diagram outlines the basics of where to stand in doubles.
		
		  1. Serving to forehand court.
		  2. Serving to backhand court.
		  3. Receiving in forehand court.
		  4. Receiving in backhand court.
		  5. One's partner serves to forehand court.
		  6. One's partner serves to backhand court.
		  7. One's partner is receiving in forehand court.

SKILL	DESCRIPTION	TEACHING TECHNIQUES AND OBSERVATION POINTS
		8. One's partner is receiving in backhand court. Note: The receiver's partner only stays in position 7 or 8 until the serve is returned. If the return goes past the net player then he or she moves to position 5 or 6 to be on attack.
	i Tactics for the Server - Usually a beginner's serve is not strong enough to follow to the net. The server should wait for a short return and then join the partner at net. The server should try to implement the following tactics:	1. Try to serve as much as possible to opponent's backhand. 2. Use cross-court strokes to keep ball away from net player. Try to keep other player at baseline. 3. After a couple of cross-court exchanges try to lob over net player in order to change the pattern. This should also give the server time to get to the net. 4. When a player is pulled up to the net by a short shot stay about four to five meters from the net. Do not get closer; remember to protect against lob. 5. When playing the net, always stay inside the service line, do not get caught back in "no man's land." 6. Person receiving a lob should try to cover it, but if partner has to come to the rescue by moving across the court, then the first person should move back to baseline to cover the half of the court that has been left empty.

	ii Tactics for the Receiver - Receiver should keep the following tactics in mind:	1. Return the service play at all costs.
		2. Try to follow the following pattern when returning serve:
		  a) Seven out of ten returns should go cross-court.
		  b) Two should be lobs.
		  c) One should be hit hard down the line past the net player to keep him or her honest.
		3. When return has kept the server back, try to get to the net.
		4. Let partner know when a lob is being played so he or she can get back to baseline.
		5. When both opponents are at net, play the ball soft and low to make them volley up.
		6. When in doubt, always hit right down the middle.
		7. Never try to win a point from the return of service. Make sure to hit the ball in so opponent has a chance to miss the return.
		8. It is the receiver's partner's duty to call the service line.

2. Advanced		

a) Singles	The game of singles in tennis is more than an athletic contest of strength, stamina, agility and skill. It is also an intellectual contest.
	
	There are three factors in the game:
	  1. mental fitness
	  2. technique -- style and skills of strokes
	  3. physical fitness
		1. Most experts agree that mental fitness is the most important requirement for winning tennis at the advanced level.
		2. Mental fitness includes.:
		  a) determination
		  b) dedication
		  c) will
		  d) courage
		  e) self-discipline

SKILL	DESCRIPTION	TEACHING TECHNIQUES AND OBSERVATION POINTS

	i Tactics - The best tactical plan is to keep opponent under constant psychological pressure.	1. Watch ball and hit it over net. The more times one can make an opponent hit the ball, the more pressure there is on this person.
		2. Play percentage tennis, waiting for the right moment to go for the "putaway" shot.
		3. Keep the ball "deep." Deep shots put more pressure on an opponent because they are harder to return and because it is difficult to start an attack when returning a deep shot.
		4. An important rule is to hit easy and wide to an opponent's strengths and hard to the weaknesses. The harder a player hits to the strengths the harder the ball is likely to come back. Don't waste energy so that opponent can use this power against you.
		5. Never concentrate totally on opponent's weakness. Playing a weakness too often may strengthen it by giving it extra practice.
		6. Develop a good serve to put pressure on the opponent.
		   a) Get the first serve in.
		   b) Keep all serves deep.
		7. Remember, errors are the killers in tennis.
		   a) In an average game of tennis sixty percent of the points are won on errors.
		   b) Only forty percent of the points are earned through placement.
		8. A good thing to remember in singles:
		   "No matches are won, but all are lost."
		Reducing errors will result in becoming a better player.

b) Doubles	Doubles is a game of position and teamwork. It is faster than singles and requires more skill, ingenuity, reflexes and touch.	
	A major difference between doubles and singles is the type of strokes used.	1. Try to hit the ball as low as possible above the net. 2. Try to hit the return of serve cross-court and keep it shallow. 3. The service and return of service comprise more than fifty percent of all strokes in doubles. The volleys and overheads make another thirty-three percent. This means that these strokes together make up more than eighty percent of the strokes used in doubles. 4. It should be fairly obvious that groundstrokes are not played very often in good doubles. 5. A good doubles player must be a good net player, server and receiver.
	Three general features of topflight tennis are:	
	i Offense	1. To win at doubles, players must attack and maintain this attack. 2. The attack position in doubles is at the net.

SKILL	DESCRIPTION	TEACHING TECHNIQUES AND OBSERVATION POINTS
ii Teamwork		1. Doubles is a team game. Teamwork begins with respect and understanding between partners. 2. Individual brilliance must be submerged and a coordinated team effort emphasized. 3. Top singles players do not necessarily make a good doubles team.
iii Anticipation		1. Play is so much faster than in singles that the anticipation of the nature and direction of strokes becomes essential. 2. Anticipation can be developed only by careful concentration on the position of the ball in respect to the player.

D. Court Conduct

Emphasize that good court conduct makes the game more enjoyable for everyone.

SKILL	DESCRIPTION	TEACHING TECHNIQUES AND OBSERVATION POINTS
1. Courtesy	Courtesy and thoughtfulness are expected at all times on and off the court.	1. Do not walk across or behind another court while a point is in progress. When trying to recover a ball or to get to a court to play, wait for an appropriate break. 2. If a ball rolls on to your court, return it promptly but in such a way as not to interrupt play on the other courts. 3. When at court-side remember that loud conversation and ball bouncing will distract players. 4. At the conclusion of a match, shake hands and thank the opponent for the game.

2. Sportsmanship	Good sportsmanship is expected at all times on and off the court. Unsportsmanlike conduct may result in a player being disqualified from a match.	1. The following are considered instances of unsportsmanlike conduct:
		   a) Outward displays of temper or racquet throwing
		   b) Obscene language or gestures and swearing
		   c) Hitting a ball in anger
		   d) Blatant "gamesmanship" or stalling
		   e) Intentional waving of a racquet or arms, mannerisms, unnatural movements, or the making of a noise in order to distract the opponent
		2. It is the responsibility of each player to call all balls fairly and honestly on his or her side of the net. When in doubt the ball should be called good.
		3. Never comment on an opponent's call unless asked.
		4. Never ask a spectator to help make a call. One player may think the spectator is qualified but the other player may not.
		5. Players must call their own double-hits, double bounces, touching the net, or reaching over the net.
		6. It is the responsibility of the server to call the score after every point.
		7. Call the ball quickly and loudly.

SKILL	DESCRIPTION	TEACHING TECHNIQUES AND OBSERVATION POINTS

3. Conduct of spectators, friends and coaches	There are some rules of conduct for people not directly involved in playing the game of tennis.	1. Parents, friends and coaches are not permitted on the court at any time.
		2. They may not volunteer advice on line calls, scoring or the conduct of the match.
		3. The following is considered poor spectator etiquette:
		   a) Applauding errors
		   b) Moving about behind the court while a point is being played
		   c) Talking loudly
		   d) Applauding or shouting out while a rally is still in progress

E. Rules

	The Canadian Lawn Tennis Association has a set of Official Playing Rules. For an up-to-date copy write to:	British Columbia Tennis Association 1200 Hornby Street Vancouver, B.C. V6Z 1W2 (For American Associations, see Appendix)
	The following information should be sufficient for beginners starting to play the game. Before the rules can be understood there are some basic terms that must be explained.	
	a) Server and Receiver	Players stand on opposite sides of the net. The player who first delivers the ball is called the server, and the other is the receiver.
	b) Permanent Fixtures	These include the net, posts and fences that surround the court.
	c) Fault	A fault is an error. If a player commits two faults on the service the opponent gets the point.
	d) Let	1. Replay of a point due to interference. 2. Examples of interference are stray balls rolling onto the court, or people from other courts moving behind or onto the court while the ball is in play. 3. The server re-serves two balls.
	e) Service Let	If the ball hits the net and goes over landing in the correct service square, that ball is re-served.
	f) Court Lines	Lines are considered part of the court. A ball touching the line is good.
	g) Choice of Sides and Service	1. The choice of ends and the right to be server or receiver in the first game shall be decided by a toss. The toss usually involves spinning the racquet - choosing rough or smooth.

SKILL	DESCRIPTION	TEACHING TECHNIQUES AND OBSERVATION POINTS

		2. The player winning the toss has the first choice and the loser has the second choice of:
		  a) The right to be server or receiver.
		  b) The choice of ends of the court.
		3. The server keeps track of the score and calls it out after every point.
		4. After a game is completed the server becomes the receiver and the receiver becomes the server. The service alternates in this manner until the end of the match.
		5. Players change ends of the court throughout the match to even out any disadvantages due to sun or wind. Whenever the total game score is odd, players switch ends of the court. After the first, third, fifth, seventh and ninth games, players alternate ends of the court.

	h) Delivery of Service	1. Server must stand outside baseline. If a player steps on or over baseline before ball is hit, or if player moves front foot before serving, it is called as a fault. 2. Server must alternate service courts. The server must start every game serving into the right hand service court from the right hand side of the court. The next point is served into the left hand service court from the left side of the court.

	i) Ball is in Play	1. Ball is in play until the point has been decided.
		2. Whenever a player commits an error the opponent wins the point. Some examples of errors are:
		  a) Player lets ball bounce twice.
		  b) Player fails to hit ball into play. Ball hits a permanent fixture outside the court.
		  c) Player hits ball more than once when stroking it.
		  d) Player touches the net with any part of the body, racquet, or clothing.
		  e) Player is hit by the ball.

F. Scoring

	Game - A game may have as few as four points or as many as hundreds.
	
	   0 - love
	   1st point - 15
	   2nd point - 30
	   3rd point - 40
	   4th point - Game
	
	40 - 40 Deuce
	
	1st point after
	  Deuce: Advantage "Ad"
	
	2nd point after
	  Deuce: Game or Deuce
		1. Have players memorize names of the points.
		2. The same person serves an entire game of tennis and is responsible for keeping track of, and calling out the score, after every point.
		3. In tennis there are always two scores, the server's score and the receiver's score.
		4. The server's score is always called first. If spectators hear the score called 40-15, they automatically know that the server is winning.
		5. A tie game, for example 40-40, is called deuce.
		6. When the score is deuce, someone must get a two point advantage (two points in a row) before the game is over.
		7. The first point after deuce is called an "Advantage." This is sometimes shortened to "Ad." The score would be called out Advantage "Ad," Server, or Advantage "Ad," Receiver, depending on who got the point.

SKILL	DESCRIPTION	TEACHING TECHNIQUES AND OBSERVATION POINTS
		8. The second point after deuce either wins the game, if the same person who won the first point wins the second, or it ties the score again at deuce, if both players get one of the points after deuce. The game continues from deuce until someone gets the two points in a row. There is no limit to the number of deuces allowed in a game of tennis so there is no limit to the number of points.
	Set - Recreational players usually play a set (six games) when they play tennis.	A set is over when one of the players has won six games with a two game advantage. The final score of a set could be 6-0, 6-4, 6-2, and so on.
	Match - Tournament players usually play a match (two out of three sets) when they play tennis.	Most tournament matches are the best two out of three sets. In some of the larger tournaments, Wimbledon or Forest Hills, men play best three out of five sets, women play best two out of three sets.

Chapter Three
Exercises

A. Flexibility

| SKILL | DESCRIPTION | TEACHING TECHNIQUES AND OBSERVATION POINTS |

Tennis helps promote physical fitness. The reverse is also true: the better one's fitness level the quicker one is likely to progress through the levels of tennis.

It is important to loosen up and warm the muscles before starting to play. This will help prevent a stretched or torn muscle if a student accidentally overextends during the activity.

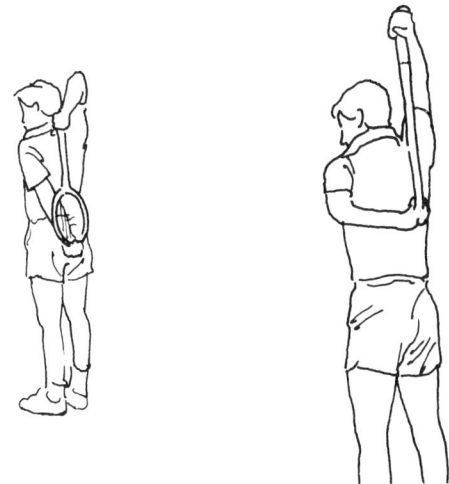

1. Arm and Shoulder

1. Grab either end of the racquet behind the back.
2. Pull gently up and down alternately with either arm.
3. Repeat.

2. Shoulder and Front of Body

1. Hold racquet with both hands, one at the head and one on the grip.
2. Stretch arms up and push them behind the body.
3. Breathe in when stretching back, breathe out when relaxing the arms.
4. Repeat.

3. Shoulder, Back and Legs

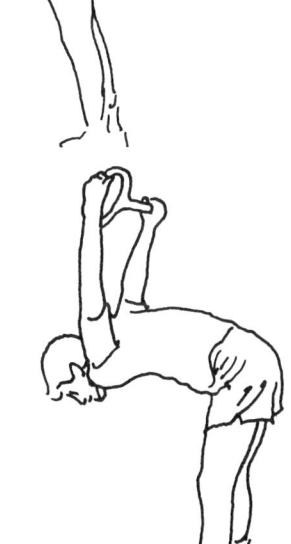

1. Hold racquet behind the back with one hand on the grip and one hand on the head.
2. Lift arms up toward head, bending slightly.
3. Repeat.

SKILL	DESCRIPTION	TEACHING TECHNIQUES AND OBSERVATION POINTS
4. Leg Stretches		1. Sit on the ground with the knees bent and hold the racquet with both hands under the feet. 2. Slowly straighten the legs to stretch the back and leg muscles. Hold for a few seconds. 3. Relax. 4. Repeat.

SKILL	DESCRIPTION	TEACHING TECHNIQUES AND OBSERVATION POINTS
5. Step-throughs		1. Hold the ends of the racquet and without letting go, step forward and then backward over the racquet. 2. Repeat.

B. Strength

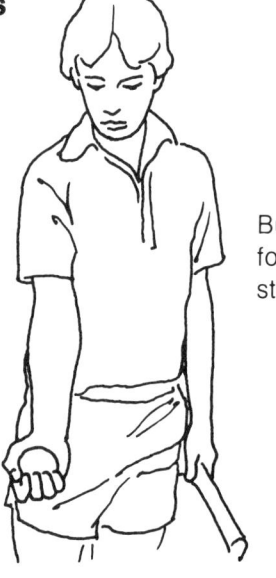

SKILL	DESCRIPTION	TEACHING TECHNIQUES AND OBSERVATION POINTS
1. Grip Isometrics	Build forearm strength.	1. Squeeze a tennis ball or the grip of the racquet and hold for about ten seconds. 2. Relax. 3. Repeat.
2. Sit-ups	Strong stomach muscles are important when serving.	1. Do bent knee sit-ups because these do not put as much pressure on the back. 2. Start at ten and work up to approximately fifty.
3. Push-ups	Arm and shoulder strength.	1. Do push-up from the toes. 2. Start with five and work up to forty.

C. Cardiovascular Fitness

SKILL	DESCRIPTION	TEACHING TECHNIQUES AND OBSERVATION POINTS
1. Skipping	Improves speed, agility, endurance and hand-eye coordination.	1. Start by skipping for about three minutes per day. 2. Build work load gradually. 3. Skip as fast as you can for the entire time.
2. Jogging	Improves stamina	1. Start slowly and gradually increase the length of the jog. 2. Fitness is important to last through long rallies and games.

Chapter Four
Drills

A. "Wimbledon Relays"

SKILL | DESCRIPTION | TEACHING TECHNIQUES AND OBSERVATION POINTS

Drills may become tedious in a large group situation. A good way to sustain interest for practice drills is to organize them into a relay meet. The drills then become games and team competitions.

Keep teams as small as possible (four to five players).

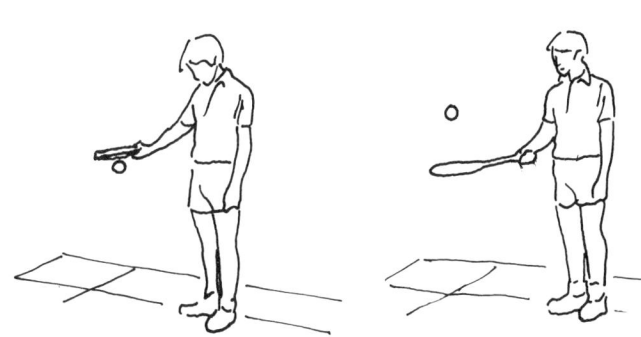

1. Racquet-Bounce-Dribble Relay
- develops hand-eye coordination
- racquet feel
- footwork

1. Arrange players in parallel lines - four to five per team.
2. Mark a turning line about thirteen meters away.
3. With the racquet, dribble the ball up to the line and back.
4. Stress proper grip and wrist position.
5. Team that finishes first wins the event.

2. Racquet-Air-Dribble Relay
- hand-eye coordination
- racquet feel
- footwork

1. Same arrangement for #1 except ball is bounced on racquet.
2. Stress proper grip, watching the ball.

3. Racquet-Air-Juggle Relay
- hand-eye coordination
- racquet feel

1. Same as #2 except ball is hit by alternate faces of the racquet.
2. Use Continental grip.

4. Racquet Balloon Carry Relay
- hand-eye coordination
- racquet feel

1. Carry or balance a balloon on the racquet face. Run to the touch line and back.
2. If balloon falls it may only be scooped up by using racquet, the hands may not touch the balloon.
3. If it is windy outside put a coin inside the balloon for added weight.

SKILL	DESCRIPTION	TEACHING TECHNIQUES AND OBSERVATION POINTS
5. Racquet-Bounce-Dribble-Skipping Relay	-footwork	1. Same as for #1, except players must skip up and back. 2. Stress proper grip and wrist position.
6. Ball-Carry Side-Skipping Relay	-footwork -forearm strength	1. Carry or balance a ball on the racquet face and skip sideways up and back to the touch line. 2. Right foot leads to turning line, left foot leads back. 3. Hold racquet with one hand.
7. Side-Skipping Touch Race	-footwork	1. Players line up between parallel lines about one and a half meters apart. 2. On "Go" signal skip sideways to touch right sideline and then back to left. 3. Count the number of times line is touched in thirty seconds. 4. Player with the highest count wins the event for team.

The following drills can be used to develop the basic tennis skills:

B. Ring-Around Rows

1. Thrower tosses four or five balls for hitter.
2. After hitting balls over net, hitter runs around to other end of court to pick up balls.
3. After picking up balls, hitter may become the thrower or may give them back to the thrower and go to end of line.

C. Drop-Hit Drill

1. Player standing in ready position drops ball and strokes it over net with a forehand groundstroke.
2. Players having difficulty may start standing sideways to the net with the preparation completed.

| SKILL | DESCRIPTION | TEACHING TECHNIQUES AND OBSERVATION POINTS |

D. Service Drill One

1. Players line up inside and outside court facing screen.
2. Practice serving into screen.
3. Targets may be attached to screen to increase challenge.

E. Service Drill Two

1. Player serves four or five balls then runs around to other end of court to pick them up.
2. Player then continues to run to end of other line.
3. Players practice ball toss while waiting for their turn to serve. The racquet may be used as a target to improve accuracy.

| SKILL | DESCRIPTION | TEACHING TECHNIQUES AND OBSERVATION POINTS |

F. "Shadowing"

Involves practicing the stroking motion without hitting the ball. "Shadowing" may be done without a racquet.

1. An important drill at the beginner level. Often at this level the stroking motion feels awkward and unnatural. Repeated practice through "shadowing" makes the stroke feel more comfortable.
2. "Shadowing" is easier than practicing hitting a ball because player does not have the judgment or timing of the ball to worry about.
3. When "shadowing" the stroke with the class, place players so they have enough room to swing freely and in such a way that the instructor can see every player.
4. When "shadowing" the stroke, instructor should face same direction as class so that the players have a model for their stroke.

Chapter Five
Sample Lesson Plans

These ten lesson plans have been developed as examples of how the skills may be taught. They cover Level I - Beginner, and introduce all the motor and cognitive aspects of the game as outlined in the activity sequence chart, Chapter One.

The lesson plans have been prepared for the following situations:

1. **Class size:** 30
2. **Facility:** Court complex, two courts and practice wall
3. **Time:** 50 minutes
4. **Equipment:** School should have thirty light-medium racquets 4 3/8" - 4 1/2" grips
School or community center should provide 100 balls per class. Where possible, players should be encouraged to have their own racquets so they can practice between classes. (See Appendix)

The lesson outlines are labeled according to the major skills introduced and developed.

The order of instruction should remain as is, but Lessons Seven and Eight have been designed to be taught in classroom settings or on the court. In case of inclement weather or facility-booking problems, they can be used at any time. If they are used early in the program every effort should be made to reinforce the subjects by on-court demonstrations or activities.

Detailed lesson plans are important in order to use time and space most effectively. The plans could serve a dual purpose:

a) They could provide an instructor's guide.
b) They could be used, in handout form, as an introduction to an entire series. This would enable the player to follow the progression, and to understand the requirements and how they will be achieved.

These sample plans are by no means rigid. They may be modified to suit circumstances such as:

a) More than one level per class.
b) Speedy progression of whole class.
c) Instructor preferences in teaching manner.

Plans such as these have proven successful in group teaching. It is important to remember to be flexible. Age and growth characteristics of players may make formation of smaller groups essential.

Lesson One - Background Material

1. Introduction - 10 min

This session will cover the essential background material. If everyone pays attention and practices with a purpose, then game skills will develop quickly. A general introduction should include a brief discussion on the following topics:

a) Why play tennis?
   i) Fun
   ii) The sport knows no boundaries to age, sex, or physical condition.
   iii) Promotes fitness - burns four to six cal./min. at a recreational level.
   iv) Sociable.
   v) Inexpensive - time and money.

b) Equipment
   i) Running shoes - explain difference between jogging and tennis shoes
   ii) Balls
   iii) Racquets - how to choose
      1) price - inexpensive
      2) wooden vs. metal
      3) grip size = average 4" - 4 1/2"
                  = measure for size
      4) weight = light to medium

c) Brief explanation of level system and lesson programs

d) Explanation of:
   i) Court = net 105 cms. high at posts 90 cms. at center
          = lines - baseline, singles and doubles, sidelines service lines
          = surface - asphalt, plexipave, cement
   ii) Terminology - forehand, backhand, service, volley, lob, overhead, groundstroke, percentage tennis (outlined in Chapter Two, Skill Development and Teaching Techniques.)

2. Objective

By the end of the lesson the players should be able to

perform the following skills:

a) Ball Sense drills
b) Ready position
c) Warm-up exercises

3. Warm-up - 10 min.

Introduce and explain the stretching exercises, using a tennis racquet. Class should be arranged in shadowing formation (see p.   ). This set-up allows instructor to see everyone with minimal movement.

Stretching warm-up: (see Chapter Three-Exercises)

a) Racquet drops behind back, grasp with opposite hand and stretch up and down
b) Holding both ends - stretch straight up
c) Stretch up behind
d) Touch toes
e) Step-through

Grip isometric: Squeezing ball or racquet. This will serve to strengthen wrist and forearm.

Players should appreciate the fact that these simple exercises can mean a faster pace of skill development.

4. Review

For Lesson One this section would be omitted, unless Lesson Seven or Eight had been used prior to Lesson One. If that is the case then a brief, verbal review of material covered would be in order.

5. New Material - 20 min.

Class arranged for shadowing, each with racquet and ball.

a) Ball sense - face partner and do toss-catch and toss-bounce-catch practice.
b) Parts of racquet
   i) head and strings
   ii) throat
   iii) grip
   iv) faces: open, neutral, closed
c) Racquet and ball drills:
   i) Forehand grip
   ii) Demonstrate how to retrieve ball
   iii) Drills   - bounce to ground
                 - bounce up on racquet
                 - reversing faces

Stress that these drills may seem silly but they develop four areas important to tennis:

   i) Hand-eye coordination
   ii) Developing feel for center of strings - sweet spot
   iii) Watching ball
   iv) Strengthening wrist and forearm

d) Demonstration and class shadowing of ready position. Stress importance of being relaxed and concentrating on imaginary ball. Get group to demonstrate.

6. Culmination/Activity

Class remains in three groups of ten. "Wimbledon Relays" - Bouncing ball on racquet around track or outside of courts, next runner must be in ready position to receive balls. Last group to finish retrieves lesson balls.

Closing remarks

a) Encouragement of ball sense drill practice.
b) Outline Lesson Two since it will get into actual tennis.

Lesson Two - Forehand

1. Introduction

This lesson will introduce and begin to develop the forehand groundstroke. It is one of the "bread and butter" shots in tennis. A good forehand can be a mainstay of anyone's game.

2. Objective

By the end of this lesson players will:

a) Demonstrate the ability to do the skills in Lesson One.
b) Have an understanding of the forehand groundstroke.
c) Be able to drop-hit a tennis ball over the net from the service line.

3. Warm-up - 5 min.

Regular routine of stretching exercises and grip isometrics as in Lesson One.

4. Review - 10 min.

Class in shadowing formation.

a) Repeat three ball sense drills, stress forehand grip.
b) Rehearse ready position.

5. New Material - 5 min.

Class in shadowing formation.

Demonstrate and explain entire forehand stroke. Class shadows.

a) Ready position
b) Preparation
c) Impact - knees lift or lower
d) Follow-through - gives depth and direction

6. Culmination/Activity - 25 min.

Arrange class for drop-hit drill. In a game situation strokes must succeed in getting ball over net.
That is, one third on wall, two thirds on courts at baselines, switch every ten minutes.
Starting with preparation complete, everyone drops ball and strokes with forehand. Correct and reinforce individuals as required.

Closing remarks: Next lesson we will develop this stroke so that movement from the ready position will be included. *Don't ignore the ball sense practice.*

Lesson Three - Forehand

1. Introduction

During this lesson the forehand groundstroke will be developed. All phases will be practiced, including movement from the ready positions. The practice will simulate actual tennis.

2. Objective

By the end of this lesson players will:

a) Be able to hit a forehand groundstroke from a tossed ball.
b) Understand "practicing with a purpose."

3. Warm-up - 5 min.

a) Regular stretching routine
b) Grip isometrics

4. Review - 10 min.

Class in shadowing formation

a) Demonstrate and class shadows forehand from ready position
b. Now add in two or three steps
   Stress - short deliberate steps
          - concentration on imaginary ball
c) Drop-hit drill refresh everyone on stroking ball.

5. New Material - 5 min.

Class in ring-around-rows drill

a) Demonstrate feeding, with two to four players shadowing.
b) Stress - early preparation, complete follow-through, concentration, return for ready position.

6. Culmination/Activity - 30 min.

Ring-around-rows forehand drill, four groups of seven, two groups per court, stroking ball in same direction. "Wimbledon Relays"

Closing remarks: Stress: Try for cross-court shots, they have four advantages:

a) Net lower at center.
b) Court is longer at diagonal so more room for error.
c) Since diagonal longer there is more time to recover.
d) Strategically sound, percentage tennis.

Lesson Four - Backhand

1. Introduction

This session will introduce the backhand groundstroke. With the two stokes done, everyone will be able to play a baseline game of tennis. The backhand is usually uncomfortable for a while but it soon becomes easy. It can be compared to the swing of a left-handed baseball batter. Everyone is probably wondering about the two-handed backhand. We will get into those during Lesson Five.

2. Objective

By the end of this lesson player will:

a) Be able to stroke a backhand from a tossed ball.
b) Have experimented with a two-handed and semi-two-handed backhand hit.

3. Warm-up - 5 min.

a) Regular stretching routine
b) Grip isometrics

4. Review - 10 min.

a) Ring-around-rows drill -forehand stroke.
b) Demonstrate forehand, stress relaxed start.

5. New Material - 15 min.

Class in shadowing formation:

a) Demonstrate backhand groundstroke:

   i) Ready position - grip change to Eastern backhand
   ii) Preparation - early; support racquet with free hand
   iii) Impact - arm close to body
   iv) Follow-through - accentuated to make up for physical limitations

b) Class shadows - correct individuals and point out common problems.

6. Culmination/Activity - 25 min.

Ring-around-rows drill, only ball feeder tosses ball exclusively to backhand.
Stress   - arm close to body
           - relaxed, smooth stroke
           - concentration on ball from feeder to impact with racquet

Closing remarks: Lesson Five continues the backhand and everyone can choose which type: single-handed, semi-, or double-handed.

Lesson Five - Backhand

1. Introduction

This lesson concludes instruction on the basic groundstrokes. Everyone must still continue to practice and develop them since they are the two basic strokes in the game.

2. Objective

By the end of this lesson players will:

a) Be able to hit forehands and backhands from a tossed ball.
b) Be able to move a few steps demonstrating correct footwork to hit forehand and backhand groundstrokes.

3. Warm-up - 5 min.
   a) Regular stretching routine
   b) Grip isometrics

4. Review - 10 min.
   a) Ring-around-rows drill
   b) Feeder throws five to forehand, five to backhand
   c) Stress - early preparation, grip change, solid impact, good follow-through
   d) Make individual corrections.

5. New Material - 10 min.

   Shadowing: introduce semi-two-handed, and two-handed backhands. Point out disadvantages:
   a) Restricts follow-through
   b) Have to be closer to ball, therefore more running
   c) Low balls hard to play
and advantages:
   a) More racquet control
   b) More power
   c) Makes up for lack of strength

6. Culmination/Activity - 25 min

10 min -
   a) Ring-around-rows drill
   b) Players trying the variations of backhand
   c) Stress picking a favorite, soon, and sticking with it.

15 min. -
   a) Ring-around-rows game - feeder randomly tosses balls to forehand and backhand, making the hitter move one or two steps.
   b) Stress concentration on ball, each player competing with group for most successful strokes in a row.

Closing remarks: Lesson Six will be the service. Some think it the most difficult stroke but it is not, it is just the most complicated. The player must now control two motions - racquet and ball toss and coordinate the two.

Lesson Six - Service

1. Introduction

The service is used to put the ball into play to start a point. The server has two attempts to start each point, and one *must* be successful or the opponent is given the point. The serve can be practiced when alone. It is the first stroke to disappear after a layoff since it requires accurate ball control and timing.

2. Objective

By the end of this lesson the player will:
   a) Be able to stroke the overhand service motion.
   b) Be able to serve ball over the net from the baseline.

3. Warm-up - 5 min.
   a) Regular stretching routine
   b) Grip isometrics

4. Review - 5 min.
   a) Ring-around-rows drill
   b) Random feeding of balls to forehand and backhand
   c) Individual corrections and demonstration when needed.

5. New Material - 10 min.

   Class in shadowing formation.
   a) Demonstrate whole service motion.
      - Stress similarity of racquet motion to that of a baseball pitcher.
      - Ball toss is like a ball placement.
   b) If necessary, break motions down and work first on the toss, then on racquet motion.
   c) Coordination of two comes from scissor motion and timing, which can only be learned by trying.

6. Culmination/Activity - 30 min.

10 min -
   a) Service drill - serving against fence.
      i) Stress relaxing, taking time to stroke.
      ii) Stress head and chin up into ball until after contact is made.
      iii) Stress developing a steady second serve. There are plenty of first serves to experiment with later.
   b) Service game - groups serving from both sides of the court, at a diagonal, across net.
      i) Stress steady placement into service court. Each player keeps track of successful serves and strives for more.

Closing remarks: All three basic strokes have been introduced. It is up to everyone to work on them. The adage "you are only as good as the number of tennis balls you hit" is important. After we get the roles, scoring, court positions, and court conduct done, there will be two stroke workshops. These will concentrate on more individual attention and will be all playing time.

Lesson Seven - Rules and Scoring

Note: There could be two approaches for this lesson; one on the court and one in a classroom setting. This plan prepares for a classroom session. If it were to be held on court then the visual aids would certainly become the court and scoring would be introduced by a game demonstration. The review would be held but as demonstration and shadowing of all the strokes. The culmination for an on-the-court session would be free play, getting used to keeping score.

1. Introduction

This session will cover the various rules and how to keep score. There are few rules and keeping score is easy once you grasp the point system. Both topics will be easy to learn when put into game situations.

2. Objective

By the end of this lesson the player will:

a) Be able to keep score in a game situation.
b) Be able to follow the appropriate rules for playing recreational and competitive tennis.

3. Warm-up - 15 min.

a) Regular stretching routine
b) Grip isometrics
c) Sit-ups   -Added to improve strength
d) Push-ups   -and to make up for wordy
e) Skipping   -lectures

4. Review - 5 min.

Discussion of what has been done to date.

5. New Material - 20 min.

Teaching aids

a) Overhead projector with permanent transparencies of court diagram.
b) Rules and scoring in handout form.

This session will center on a discussion of rules and scoring as outlined in Chapter Two, Skill Development and Teaching Techniques.

6. Culmination/Activity - 10 min.

Two choices:

a) Film of world class tennis players. Available from Tennis Association Offices (See Appendix.)
b) Jogging

Lesson Eight - Court Positions and Court Conduct

1. Introduction

The last area of background knowledge required for this sport is rules on conduct, court positions, and basic strategy for singles and doubles.

2. Objective

By the end of this lesson the player will:

a) Be able to demonstrate the basic court positions.
b) Be able to discuss court conduct and singles and doubles strategy.

3. Warm-up - 15 min.

a) Regular stretching routine
b) Grip isometrics
c) Sit-ups
d) Push-ups
e) Skipping

4. Review

Discussion of what has been done to date.

5. New Material - 20 min.

Teaching aids

a) Overhead projector, court diagram transparencies.
b) Conduct, positions, strategies in handout form.

This session will focus on the court positions, conduct, and simple strategies as outlined in Chapter Two, Skill Development and Teaching Techniques.

6. Culmination/Activity - 10 min.

Two alternatives:

a) Jogging
b) Film on tennis; even video recording of T.V. tennis would be excellent to inspire players.

Lesson Nine and Lesson Ten - Game Workshops

Note: This plan will serve both the final sessions.

1. Introduction

These game workshops will be sessions of playing tennis. They give the instructor an opportunity to examine the player's progress. It is also a perfect time for them to become aware of their own weaknesses and get individual attention to correct them before bad habits develop.

The teaching program itself may be evaluated as well.

2. Objective

By the end of these lessons players will be able to:

a) Analyze their strokes for weaknesses.
b) Play games for enjoyment.
c) Be evaluated in all the areas they have covered in the lessons.

3. Warm-up - 5 min.

a) Regular stretching routine
b) Grip isometrics

At this point the class is divided, one half playing tennis, the other half playing baseball using a tennis ball and a racquet as a bat.

4. Review

Omitted to allow as much time as possible for tennis game.

5. New Material

Omitted to allow as much time as possible for tennis game.

6. Culmination/Activity - 45 min.

Each group would normally be fifteen players.

Group A   - Baseball using racquet and ball.
          - Underhand pitching, old tennis racquet.

Group B   1. Seven players on courts for doubles. Instructor participates.
          2. Rotation with eight others, who are practicing on wall, every three complete games.

Assuming rotation every fifteen minutes, everyone

should get to play nine supervised games, with different partners and opponents.

Closing remarks: That concludes Level I. Everyone is now past the beginner stage and must keep at it because the next levels are where they will notice rapid improvement in their tennis abilities. Now that the basic skills are there, all of one's concentration can be applied to the ball.

Players input into the tennis program should be invited at this time.

Lesson Eleven - Multiple Skill Levels

1. Introduction

This sample lesson plan deals with a class comprised of players at various levels of skill development. This situation might arise if players have participated in summer tennis programs or might result from individual learning rates.

This lesson will deal with twenty Level I, six Level II and four Level III, players. It is assumed that the Level I players will be nearing completion of that level.

2. Objective

This lesson requires multiple objectives:

a) The Level I players will develop groundstrokes.
b) The Level II players will be able to serve with more consistency and control.
c) The Level III players will develop ball control skills by being teaching assistants.

3. Warm-up - 10 min.

The class is separated into two groups which will be led through the exercise routine by two Level III players. The warm-up consists of:

a) Regular stretching routine
b) Grip isometrics
c) Sit-ups
d) Push-ups
e) Skipping

4. Review

Short discussion of reason for group separations. Important point to consider is that the Level I players will benefit from Level IIIs feeding tennis balls for groundstroke practice. This drill takes skill very close to game situations. The Level II players will have more individual attention to iron out service problems.

5. New Material - 5 min.

Explanation of drill procedure.

Ten Level I players arranged in two lines of five, at baseline. A Level III player puts ball into play from opposite baseline. Feeding should be reasonably precise and rapid, alternating sides of court to keep line moving from forehand to backhand. Other Level III player feeds balls to the other group of five. Each Level I player hits four of each stroke then retrieves ball. This is repeated on court two with the others.

The Level II players are arranged along a practice wall for serving drill. The purpose is to serve for control, develop form, and strengthen serving arm. The instructor makes individual corrections.

6. Culmination/Activity - 30 min.

The groups remain as established, but now each player is asked to set a goal. It could be for a number of strokes in a row or successful serves towards a target taped to the wall. The Level III players should strive towards consecutive balls fed to a specific spot.

Goals should be individual and attainable in thirty minutes. Players should be encouraged to record results, practice on their own, and repeat this game.

Closing remarks: This program illustrates that players with various skill levels can work together with improvement for everyone.

Chapter Six
Evaluation

This tennis handbook has been developed assuming that all players will start at Level I - Beginner. No evaluation is necessary for entry into the program. However, if players have had some experience with tennis, initial evaluation would have to occur. Test (See p.47) could be used to determine entry level.

At the initial stages of instruction, evaluation may be geared to ensure that the player is not overly criticized or discouraged. There are enough technical aspects to consider: correction of every aspect of the player's ability is unnecessary.

A prime objective in teaching tennis is to offer an enjoyable lifetime activity. To motivate players and to keep them interested in the game outside classroom time, it may be more important to allow them to be challenged by skills at a higher level without completing all lower level skills. This is a decision that individual instructors will have to make.

A. Program Evaluation

The success of the program can be judged by the players' response, their progress rate and how much they enjoy playing the game. Their enjoyment may be determined by the extent of participation outside of Physical Education class time. The number of players who turn out for the school tennis club or team, or for social round-robins organized after school and at noon hours, would be a good indication of success.

B. Player Evaluation

Player evaluation should incorporate the psychomotor, cognitive and affective objectives as outlined in Chapter One.

1. Psychomotor:

Three general standards by which to evaluate psychomotor skill progress may be used by the instructor as well as the player. These are in order of relative importance:

  a) **Efficiency:** Slight modifications of standard form are certainly acceptable if the stroke is successful.
  b) **Economy:** Control of movement, body and racquet, positioning and reactions are essential to produce strokes which "get the job done" without undue waste of time or effort.
  c) **Style:** There is not one strict way to perform a skill. Everyone is different, and individuality will surface. Form in skills is somewhat flexible and still allows for variation yet "proper" stroke production.

After the basic skills are developed, generally at the intermediate level, the instructor can be more demanding in the evaluation of stroke production. Strokes may be analyzed from three points of view -- to gauge the player's ability, to find and correct problem areas, and to examine teaching weaknesses.

 a) **Stroke Evaluation**
  Tennis strokes may be evaluated by the five fundamentals of stroke production:

  1. **The ball:** Seventy percent of mistakes result from poor concentration. The player must watch and see the ball as long as it is in play.
  2. **Correct footwork:** Movement in tennis requires good body control. Short, deliberate steps, good court positioning, and early preparation are the keys to successful shots and recovering to make the next one.
  3. **Correct control of the racquet head:** The racquet head is the first line of contact with the ball. Two controlling factors are:
     a) Wrist: firm on the groundstrokes and volley: broken on serve and overhead.
     b) Grip: the angle of the racquet face is determined by the grip. Appropriate grips must be used for individual strokes.
  4. **Correct motion of the racquet:** The racquet must travel through the ball in smooth, flowing stroke corridors.
  5. **Good balance and weight transfer:** The phrase "coordinated harmony" is most apt here. The strength and steadiness of strokes comes from smooth and controlled weight transfer. Jumping at the ball causes loss of control and usually results in weak, inaccurate shots.

Evaluating a player's general ability by these five fundamentals can be an asset in discovering problems, especially if the instructor cannot spot small technical flaws.

 b) **Visual Assessment**
  A general technique for evaluation would be visual assessment: spotting mistakes, suggesting remedies, and then re-checking. A checklist of name and skills could be kept by the instructor or even by the player. An advanced palyer may assist the instructor in visual assessment.

As a player develops, this visual check could be combined with an oral approach. After seeing a mistake the instructor could check to find out if the player was aware of it and of how to correct it. This can help the player to become more aware of the ball and of stroke production.

2. Cognitive:

Specific questions should indicate how knowledgeable the player is regarding the game of tennis. The questions could take the form of an oral or written quiz. For example:

a) Define percentage tennis.

b) How is the service decided?

c) How does one keep score in tennis?

d) What are the advantages and disadvantages of the two-handed backhand?

3. Affective:

A player's affective or "social" skills are just as important as the cognitive and psychomotor skills and deserve attention during evaluation. Although affective skills may be *observed* from one session to the next, a few sample questions may assist in the evaluation. For example:

a) What is a player's attitude toward losing?

b) What is "gamemanship"?

c) Have players participated in the sessions to the best of their ability?

d) How does a player conduct himself or herself on the court?

e) Do players have a positive attitude toward the game?

Appendix I
Reference Materials

A. Books

Brabenec, Josef. *Tennis: The Game for Everyone.*
Vancouver: British Columbia Tennis Association, 1972.

Braden, Vic., Burns, Bill. *Tennis For The Future.*
Toronto: Little, Brown & Company, 1972.

Gallwey, Timothy W. *Inner Tennis.*
New York: Random House, 1974.

Kramer, Jack. *How To Play Your Best Tennis.*
New York: Atheneum/Smi, 1977.

B. Periodicals

Racquets Canada, 643 Yonge St., Toronto, Ontario, M4Y 2A2

World Tennis, 15 Love St., Marion, Ohio, U.S.A. 43302

C. Films

Provincial Educational Media Centre
7451 Elmbridge Way
Richmond, B.C.
  Ralston, Dennis. Tennis Films.
  Tennis Basics: The Forehand
  Tennis Basics: The Backhand
  Tennis Basics: The Serve
  Tennis Basics: The Volley

D. Tennis Associations

Canadian Lawn Tennis Association
Association Canadienne de Lawn Tennis
#333 River Road
Vanier, Ontario
K1L 8B9

British Columbia Tennis Association
1200 Hornby Street
Vancouver, B.C.
V6Z 1W2

United States Tennis Association
51 East 42nd Street
New York, New York   10017

United States Professional Tennis Association
Colony Beach Hotel
1620 Gulf Of Mexico Drive
Dept. G
Sarasota, Long Beach Key
Florida   33548

Appendix II
Equipment

Three basic pieces of tennis equipment are: shoes, racquets, and balls.

Tennis shoes should be dealt with because of the pounding one's feet take on the court. Tennis shoes should have good side support and traction. A common mistake is that players wear jogging shoes which are not conducive to quick sideways movement.

Tennis balls are certainly the major expense. A program using the ten sample lesson plans would require approximately 100 - 120 optic yellow, heavy duty tennis balls. These could be the pressurized or or pressureless variety. To help reduce cost, buy used tennis balls from the various clubs or tournaments. Once-used balls can often be bought for fifty percent of their original value.

Tennis racquets may be player-supplied but they should have some guidance before buying one. Some important considerations are:
  a) Wooden racquets accent control; metal ones highlight power. Wood is better for beginners.
  b) Price: $8.00 - $12.00 buys a good wooden starter racquet.
  c) It should have a leather, not vinyl, grip and nylon strings.
  d) Grip Size: measure from tip of index finger to intersect with longest palm crease, this gives grip size usually between 10 - 12 cm.
  e) Weight: light to medium according to wrist and forearm strength.

Appendix III
CTA Examiner's Test Sheet & CTA Levels Test

The Canadian Tennis Performance Awards Scheme Examiner's Test Sheet is added so that instructors may compare it to the test in the manual. The test in the manual covers all the areas but is shorter because it combines one or two of the levels to conform to the handbook format.

Canadian Tennis Association Levels Test

An objective way to evaluate players has been developed by the Canadian Tennis Association which has set out a series of tests designed to assess a player's ability to perform the basic tennis skills. The tests were also intended to motivate young players to improve their skills and to increase their understanding of the rules and the code of conduct of the game.

The test can be used in a class situation to assess the players' readiness for entry into the next level of skills.

Level I - Beginner

1. *Bounce Ball From Racquet to Ground*
   a) To pass, this must be done 30 times consecutively.
   b) Player must have a reasonable forehand grip.
   c) The ball must be under control.

2. *Bounce Ball Up on Racquet*
   a) To pass, this must be done 20 times consecutively.
   b) Same rules as for #1

3. *Forehands From a Dropped Ball*
   a) The teacher drops the ball and the player strokes forehands over the net and into the singles court.
   b) A player has ten attempts and must be successful on at least six to pass.

4. *Backhands from a Dropped Ball*
   Same as #3, except player uses backhands.

5. *Service Toss*
   The player stands in the correct service position and, using the service toss action, attempts to land the ball in a circle of a 60 cm. radius situated on the ground just inside the service court and opposite the hitting shoulder.

6. *Bounce Ball Up on Racquet Alternating Faces*
   Using the Continental grip, the player attempts to bounce the ball up 20 consecutive times alternating the faces of the racquet. The ball must be under control.

7. *Forehands From a Tossed Ball*
   Starting from a ready position the player strokes forehands over the net into the singles court. Ten balls are tossed underhand. To pass, a player must succeed in at least seven.

8. *Backhands From a Tossed Ball*
   Same as for #7, except player uses backhand.

9. *Alternate Forehands and Backhands From a Tossed Ball*
   Same for #7 and #8, except that the ball is tossed to forehands and backhands alternately.

10. *Serving*
    Using the full service motion the player serves from outside the baseline. The ball must go over the net and land anywhere in the singles court. A player must succeed in seven of the ten attempts.

11. *Basic Rules and Code of Conduct*
    a) A player must answer correctly seven out of ten questions on the basic rules of tennis and code of conduct.
    b) Questions are given orally.

Level II - Novice

1. *Rally With Tester on Forehand*
   a) Player rallies forehands with the tester and keeps the ball in play over the net and into the court.
   b) All strokes must be made after one bounce.
   c) To pass, a player must hit ten consecutive returns.

2. *Rally With Tester on Backhand*
   Same as for #1, except player uses backhand.

3. *Serving*
   a) Using the full service motion, a player serves ten balls, five from the right side and five from the left side of the court outside the baseline.
   b) To pass, a player must make seven out of ten serves into the correct service area.

4. *Forehand Volley*
   a) Beginning in the volley ready position, a player must hit forehand volleys over the net and into the court.
   b) The ball is racquet-fed by teacher.
   c) To pass, the player must hit seven out of ten into the court.

5. *Backhand Volley*
   Same as for #4, except player uses backhand.

6. *Rally With Tester Mixing Forehands and Backhands*
   Same as #1 and #2, except forehands and backhands are mixed.

7. *Forehand and Backhand Volleys*
   Same as #4, except thrower mixes the tosses to the forehands and backhands.

8. *Lob*
   a) Starting from baseline, the player attempts to lob balls into the back court beyond the service line.
   b) The balls are racquet-fed by tester.
   c) To pass, a player must succeed in seven out of ten.

9. *Court Etiquette and Rules*
   a) Student must answer correctly four out of five questions pertaining to court etiquette and rules.
   b) Questions are given orally.

10. *Basic Court Positions*
    a) Student must answer correctly four out of five questions pertaining to basic court positions in doubles and singles.
    b) Questions are given orally.

Level III - Intermediate

1. *Deep Forehands*
   a) Player rallies forehands with the tester and keeps the ball deep in the court so that it lands beyond the service line.
   b) To pass, a player must succeed in seven out of ten.

2. *Deep Backhands*
   Same as for #1, except using backhand.

3. *Overheads*
   a) Starting from a volley ready position at the net, the student attempts overheads off lobs no deeper than the service line.
   b) Balls are racquet-fed by the tester.
   c) To pass, a player must succeed in seven out of ten tries.

4. *Forehand Volley From a Strokes Ball*
   a) From a volley ready position at the net, player hits forehand volleys over the net and into the court.
   b) Balls are racquet-fed by the tester.
   c) To pass, player must succeed in seven out of ten.

5. *Backhand Volley From a Stroked Ball*
   Same as for #4, except on the backhand.

Level IV - Tournament (Advanced)

1. *Cross-Court Placement*
   a) Starting from a ready position at the middle of the baseline, the player has five attempts to move to the forehand side and stroke the ball cross-court.
   b) The player has five more tries on the backhand side.
   c) The balls are racquet-fed by the tester.
   d) To pass, a player must succeed in seven out of ten.

2. *Down the Line*
   a) Starting from a ready position on the center of the baseline, the player moves to the forehand side and strokes the ball down the line into the court beyond the service line.
   b) Player does same test on the backhand side.
   c) Player has five attempts on each side and must be successful in seven out of ten.

3. *Forehand and Backhand Volleys*
   a) Starting in a volley ready position at net, the player rallies forehand and backhand volleys back to the tester.
   b) Tester mixes balls to both forehand and backhand.
   c) Out of ten volleys the player must be successful in seven.

4. *Return of Serve*
   a) Starting in a ready position at appropriate spot, the player must return serves over the net and into the singles court.
   b) Medium-paced balls are served by the tester.
   c) To pass, a player must be successful in seven out of ten.

5. *Overheads*
   a) From a volley ready position at the net a player must move back and smash lobs which fall deeper than the service line.
   b) To pass, the player must succeed in seven out of ten.

6. *Cross-Court - Down the Line Placement*
   a) Starting in a ready position at the center of the baseline, a player has six attempts on the forehand side to hit alternately cross-court and down the line shots deeper than the service line.
   b) Player has six tries on the backhand side.
   c) The balls are racquet-fed by the tester.
   d) To pass, a player must succeed in eight out of twelve.

Sports Handbook Series

Tennis Handbook
Graphics illustrate grips and strokes in this compact guide to a popular sport. Everything necessary to teach - and play - is tucked between the covers.
ISBN 0-88839-049-1 $5.95

Folk Dance Handbook
The fascinating complexities of this activity are set out in a clear, easy-to-follow format that should bring the delights of folk dance within the reach of everyone.
ISBN 0-88839-044-0 $8.95

Soccer Handbook
Skills and how to teach them; drills and when to use them; plus detailed plans for sequential teaching of the game. Compact yet comprehensive.
ISBN 0-88839-048-3 $6.95

Field Hockey Handbook
Concise, clearly illustrated, a useful guide to learning and teaching a fast-growing sport.
ISBN 0-88839-043-2 $8.95

Basketball Handbook
Rules and activities are clearly illustrated to make this guide indispensable to anyone coaching or teaching the game.
ISBN 0-88839-042-4 $8.95

Badminton Handbook
A well-illustrated guide to all the basics of the game, this also includes a discussion of teaching strategies when player skills vary widely.
ISBN 0-88839-041-6 $5.95

Men's Gymnastics Handbook
Teaching sequences for the six Olympic events of men's artistic gymnastics are explained in detail, with precise information on spotting and safety techniques providing valuable guidance for the instructor.
ISBN 0-88839-046-7 $16.95

Women's Gymnastics Handbook
A detailed guide to the teaching of gymnastic skills for women, including lesson plans and methods for evaluating performers.
ISBN 0-88839-045-9 $12.95

Orienteering Handbook
The rapidly-growing interest in this activity makes the publication of this book particularly timely. It includes detailed information on basic concepts, setting a course and organizing a meet, as well as addresses for obtaining equipment and other resources.
ISBN 0-88839-047-5 $5.95

ALSO AVAILABLE

Safety in Gymnastics *by Gerald A. Carr PhD.* A comprehensive guide to spotting and safety techniques in the gymnasium. 600 sequential illustrations. ISBN 0-99939-054-8 $12.95.

Curling Handbook *by Roy D. Theissen.* The history of the game, complete, detailed. ISBN 0-919654-71-1 $5.95

Tennis: The Decision-Making Sport *by Josef Brabenec.* Think your way to victory on the court with Canada's national tennis coach. ISBN 0-88839-052-1 $9.95

Send check or money order to:
HANCOCK HOUSE PUBLISHERS
1431 Harrison Avenue, Blaine, WA, U.S.A. 98230
HANCOCK HOUSE PUBLISHERS LTD.
19313 Zero Avenue, Surrey, B.C., Canada V3S 5J9